Fact Finders™

Questions and Answers: Countries

Brazil

A Question and Answer Book

by Brandy Bauer

Consultant:
Colin M. MacLachlan
John Christy Barr Distinguished Professor of History
Tulane University
New Orleans, Louisiana

Capstone press

Mankato, Minnesota

Fact Finders is published by Capstone Press,
151 Good Counsel Drive, P.O. Box 669, Mankato, Minnesota 56002.
www.capstonepress.com

Library of Congress Cataloging-in-Publication Data
Bauer, Brandy.
    Brazil: a question and answer book / by Brandy Bauer.
    p. cm.—(Fact finders. Questions and answers. Countries)
    Includes bibliographical references.
    ISBN-10: 0-7368-2481-2 (hardcover)
    ISBN-13: 978-1-4296-0218-1 (softcover pbk.)
    ISBN-10: 1-4296-0218-X (softcover pbk.)
    1. Brazil—Juvenile literature. I. Title. II. Series.
F2508.5.B38 2005b
981—dc22   2004021784

Summary: Describes the geography, history, economy, and culture of Brazil in a
question-and-answer format.

Editorial Credits
Christine Peterson, editor; Kia Adams, series designer; Jennifer Bergstrom, book designer;
maps.com, map illustrator; Wanda Winch, photo researcher; Scott Thoms, photo editor;
Eric Kudalis, product planning editor

Photo Credits
Art Directors/Jeff Greenberg, 24 (bottom); Banco Central do Brasil, 29 (top, coins); Bruce
Coleman Inc./Joachim Messerschmidt, 9; Bruce Coleman Inc./John Giustina, 4; Bruce
Coleman Inc./Luis Villota, 23; Capstone Press Archives, 29 (top, paper currency); Corbis,
cover (background); Corbis/Archive Iconografico, S. A., 7; Corbis/Reuters NewMedia Inc.,
19; Corbis/Stephanie Maze, 15, 24–25; Doranne Jacobson, 12–13; Escola do Parque da
Cidade (PROEM), Brasilia-DF, Brasil/LTNet-Brasil/Vera Suguri, 16–17; Houserstock/Steve
Cohen, 11; Index Stock Imagery/Jeff Dunn, cover (foreground); Photodisc/John Wang, 1;
StockHaus Limited, 29 (bottom); Victor Englebert, 16 (bottom), 21; Wolfgang Kaehler, 27

Artistic Effects
Photodisc/Jules Frazier, 18 (soccer ball)

1 2 3 4 5 6 10 09 08 07 06 05

Table of Contents

Features

Where is Brazil?

Brazil is the largest country in South America. It is the fifth largest country in the world. Brazil is about the same size as the **continental** United States.

The Amazon **rain forest** is Brazil's most famous landform. This tropical area is the world's largest rain forest. The Amazon River flows through the rain forest and across northern Brazil.

The Amazon River flows for 3,990 miles (6,421 kilometers). It is the second longest river in the world. ▶

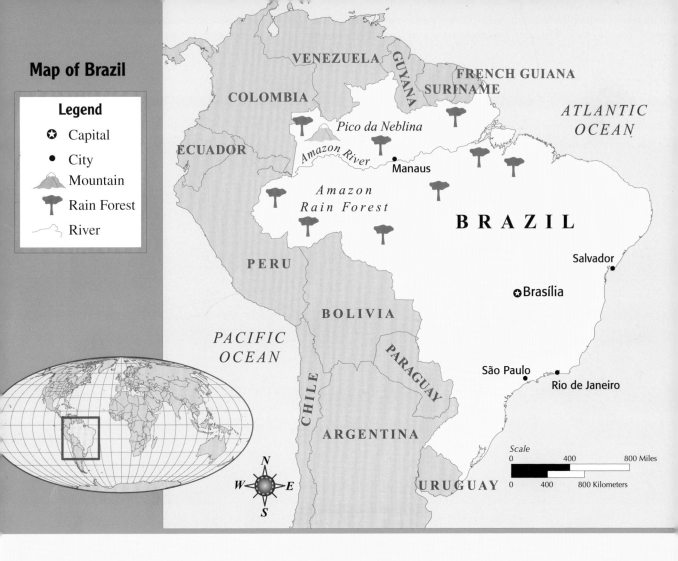

Map of Brazil

Legend

- ✪ Capital
- • City
- 🏔 Mountain
- 🌳 Rain Forest
- 〜 River

VENEZUELA

GUYANA

FRENCH GUIANA

SURINAME

COLOMBIA

ATLANTIC OCEAN

ECUADOR

Pico da Neblina

Amazon River

Manaus

Amazon Rain Forest

BRAZIL

PERU

Salvador

Brasília

BOLIVIA

PACIFIC OCEAN

PARAGUAY

São Paulo

Rio de Janeiro

CHILE

ARGENTINA

Scale

0   400   800 Miles

0   400   800 Kilometers

URUGUAY

N W E S

Brazil's eastern coast stretches along the Atlantic Ocean for almost 4,800 miles (7,700 kilometers). This area is known for its long sandy beaches.

5

When did Brazil become a country?

Brazil became an independent nation on September 7, 1822. Before then, Brazil had been a **colony** of Portugal. The Portuguese ruled Brazil from 1500 until 1822. That year, Dom Pedro I declared Brazil free from Portugal's control and became **emperor**.

Dom Pedro I ruled Brazil for nine years. His son Dom Pedro II then ruled the country. In 1889, new leaders took control of Brazil. They named the country the Federative **Republic** of Brazil.

Fact!

The Portuguese used native Brazilians and Africans as slaves. In the 1800s, there were about 3 million slaves in Brazil. Slavery in Brazil ended in 1888.

In 1822, Dom Pedro I, in uniform, greeted a crowd after he declared Brazil's independence from Portugal.

In 1964, Brazil's army took over the country. Army leaders ruled Brazil until 1985. In 1985, new leaders came to power in Brazil. They wanted people in Brazil to choose their own leaders.

What type of government does Brazil have?

Brazil's government is a federative republic. This system of government is like the U.S. government in many ways. In both countries, people elect a president and other leaders. The president leads the country. Brazil's president serves a four-year term.

People in Brazil elect leaders to serve in the National Congress. This group is like the U.S. Congress. The National Congress meets in the capital city of Brasília.

Fact!

Brazil's Senate has 81 members. The Chamber of Deputies has 513 members.

The National Congress buildings are located in Brasília.

The National Congress has two parts. They are the Federal Senate and the Chamber of Deputies. These two groups work together to write and pass new laws for Brazil.

What kind of housing does Brazil have?

Most Brazilians live in big cities on the coast. They live in apartments or small houses. Rich people live in large houses.

About 11 million people live in or near the rain forest. Many of these people live in small cities. They make their homes from stone, wood, or plants.

Where do people in Brazil live?

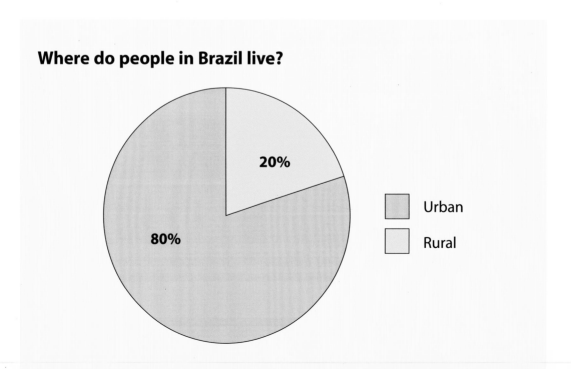

20%

80%

Urban

Rural

Millions of Brazilians live in favelas outside of large cities.

Many poor Brazilians live in favelas. Favelas are groups of small houses, usually located near large cities. These houses are made of plywood, tin, or cardboard. Many of these houses do not have electricity or running water.

What are Brazil's forms of transportation?

People in Brazil use many forms of transportation. Brazil has roads in most parts of the country. People ride buses, cars, and taxis to work. In larger cities, people also ride subways.

Boats carry people and goods. Smaller boats carry people and goods along rivers. On the coast, ships carry people to and from other countries.

Fact!

The Trans-Amazon Highway cuts across Brazil for about 3,000 miles (4,800 kilometers). People use the road to carry goods through the rain forest.

Brazil has many railroads and airports. At least 18,640 miles (30,000 kilometers) of railroads cut across the country. Trains carry most goods across Brazil. Brazil also has about 3,300 airports.

What are Brazil's major industries?

Agriculture is a major industry in Brazil. Many cattle ranches cover the southern part of the country. Brazil **exports** more coffee and tobacco than any other country. Brazil also exports soybeans and sugar. Corn, oranges, rice, and nuts are other main crops.

Many Brazilians work in factories. Brazil is one of the world's largest carmakers. Brazilian workers also make shoes, airplanes, rubber, and furniture.

What does Brazil import and export?

Imports	Exports
chemicals	coffee
electrical equipment	gems
machinery	soybeans
	tobacco

Soybeans are becoming a major industry in Brazil.

Mining is a large industry in Brazil. Most of the world's gems are mined there. People also mine gold in parts of the country. Brazil has large amounts of iron ore and bauxite.

What is school like in Brazil?

In Brazil, all children between ages 7 and 14 must go to school. Grade school lasts for eight years. Most students then go to high school and college.

For most students, school begins at 7:00 in the morning. Classes end at noon. Students have summer vacation in January or February.

Schools outside Brazil's large cities often are small and have few supplies for children. ➤

Outside the cities, students go to school in one-room buildings. Many poor children drop out of school to work.

The Brazilian government is working to help poor children stay in school. The government pays poor families if their children go to school most of the time.

What are Brazil's favorite sports and games?

Soccer is the most popular sport in Brazil. Brazilians of all ages play soccer year-round. Brazil has won four World Cup soccer titles. Brazilian Edson Arantes Nascimento, also known as Pelé, is one of the world's most famous soccer players.

People enjoy many other sports and games. Basketball is played at schools. People also play tennis and chess.

Fact!

Brazil's Pelé scored 1,281 goals in 22 years of playing soccer.

The Brazilian women's soccer team competes in many events around the world.

People in Brazil take part in many outdoor activities. People enjoy swimming, surfing, and playing volleyball at Brazil's many beaches. People also like to hike and climb Brazil's hills and mountains.

What are the traditional art forms in Brazil?

The samba is the national music and dance of Brazil. Brazilians invented samba music. It has African beats. The dance was created to go with the music.

Weaving is a popular art form in the rain forest. People use grasses, plants, and tree bark to make baskets. People also weave hammocks to use as beds.

Fact!

Christ the Redeemer is a famous statue in Rio de Janeiro. It stands 98 feet (30 meters) tall. The statue sits on a mountain above the city.

Brazil's Yanomami Indians weave baskets from rain forest plants.

People in Brazil enjoy other art forms. Books by Brazilian writers are printed in many languages. Painting, sculpture, and movies are also popular.

What major holidays do people in Brazil celebrate?

Carnival is the most famous holiday in Brazil. Carnival is held in February or March before the Christian season of **Lent**. During carnival, dancers and other performers fill the streets for parades. People often wear colorful costumes.

Brazilians celebrate national holidays. On September 7, they celebrate Brazil's freedom from Portugal. On November 15, people honor the day Brazil became a republic.

What other holidays do people in Brazil celebrate?

Children's Day
Labor Day
New Year's Day

During carnival, Brazilians fill the streets to watch the many parades.

Christian holidays are also important. People celebrate Good Friday, Easter, All Souls' Day, and Christmas. On October 12, Brazilians honor the country's **patron saint**, Our Lady of Aparecida.

What are the traditional foods of Brazil?

Manioc flour, black beans, and rice are common foods in Brazil. Manioc flour is made from a plant that grows in the rain forest. People also eat meat, fish, and fresh fruits and vegetables.

Coffee is part of every Brazilian meal. Brazilians like their coffee sweet. Many people add sugar to their coffee.

Rice and seafood are popular dishes at Brazilian restaurants. ➤

People in Brazil eat fresh fruits, vegetables, and seafood, such as squid.

Many foods come from Brazil's Indian, Portuguese, and African cultures. The country's most popular dish is a bean and meat stew called *feijoada*. African slaves first made this stew.

What is family life like in Brazil?

Brazilian families are smaller today than in the past. Years ago, many families had five or six children. Now, most families have two children.

Poor children often have hard lives. Some children do not have homes. Others beg or work to earn money for their families.

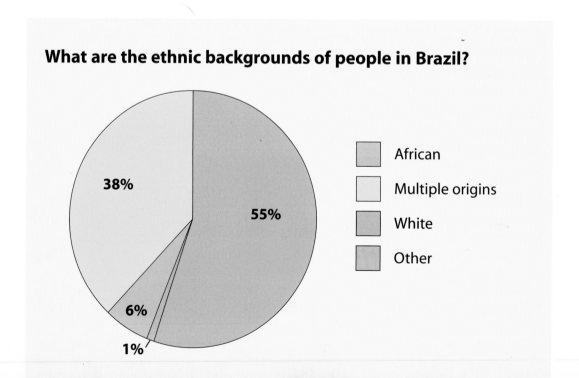

What are the ethnic backgrounds of people in Brazil?

- 38%
- 55%
- 6%
- 1%

- African
- Multiple origins
- White
- Other

Brazilian families enjoy spending time together.

Brazilian families are very close. Many children live with their parents until they get married. Aunts, uncles, and grandparents often live nearby.

Brazil Fast Facts

Official name:

Federative Republic of Brazil

Land area:

3,265,058 square miles
(8,456, 500 square kilometers)

**Average annual
precipitation (Brasília):**

63 inches (160 centimeters)

**Average January
temperature (Brasília):**

70 degrees Fahrenheit
(21 degrees Celsius)

**Average July
temperature (Brasília):**

65 degrees Fahrenheit
(18 degrees Celsius)

Population:

182,032,604 people

Capital city:

Brasília

Language:

Portuguese

Natural resources:

bauxite, forests, gold, iron ore

Religions:

Roman Catholic   80%
Other   20%

Money and Flag

Money:

Brazil's money is the real. In 2004, 1 U.S. dollar equaled 2.84 Brazilian reals. One Canadian dollar equaled 2.22 Brazilian reals.

Flag:

Brazil's flag is green with a yellow diamond and blue globe in the center. There are 27 stars on the globe. A white banner on the globe has the words Ordem E Progresso, *which means "Order and Progress," written across the front. The colors green and yellow represent Brazil's forests and minerals. Blue and white are the colors of Portugal.*

Learn to Speak Portuguese

Most people in Brazil speak Portuguese. It is the official language of Brazil. Learn to speak some Portuguese using the words below.

English	Portuguese	Pronunciation
hello	oi	(OY)
good-bye	tchau	(CHOW)
yes	sim	(SEEM)
no	não	(NOU)
please	por favor	(POR fah-VOR)
thank you	obrigado	(O-bree-GAH-doh)
you're welcome	de nada	(CHUH NAH-dah)

Glossary

colony (KOL-uh-nee)—an area that is settled and ruled by people from another country

continental (KON-tuh-nen-tuhl)—part of a continent; the continental United States is made up of the 48 states not including Hawaii or Alaska.

emperor (EM-pur-ur)—the male ruler of an area called an empire

export (EKS-port)—to send and sell goods to other countries

Lent (LENT)—the 40 days before Easter in the Christian church year

manioc (ma-NEE-ock)— a plant grown in the rain forest with starchy roots that can be made into flour

patron saint (PAY-trun SAYNT)—a saint in the church to whom a person or place is dedicated

rain forest (RAYN FOR–ist)—a tropical woodland that gets at least 100 inches (254 centimeters) of rain each year

republic (ree-PUHB-lik)—a government headed by a president with officials elected by the people

Internet Sites

FactHound offers a safe, fun way to find Internet sites related to this book. All of the sites on FactHound have been researched by our staff.

Here's how:
1. Visit *www.facthound.com*
2. Type in this special code **0736824812** for age-appropriate sites. Or enter a search word related to this book for a more general search.
3. Click on the **Fetch It** button.

FactHound will fetch the best sites for you!

Read More

Fontes, Justine, and Ron Fontes. *Brazil.* A to Z. New York: Children's Press, 2003.

Gray, Shirley W. *Brazil.* First Reports. Minneapolis: Compass Point Books, 2001.

Park, Ted. *Taking Your Camera to Brazil.* Austin, Texas: Steadwell Books, 2000.

Index